The Days of Echoes Past

Hope through the Storm

R. Joseph Romero

ISBN 978-1-0980-5712-1 (paperback)
ISBN 978-1-0980-5713-8 (digital)

Christian Faith Publishing, Inc.
832 Park Avenue
Meadville, PA 16335
www.christianfaithpublishing.com

Cover photo by: Ron Romero
Author Photo by: Chenoa Sedillo
(Etniefaith@gmail.com)

Printed in the United States of America

This work is dedicated to our children: Matthew, Feliz, Nathan, Ryan, Jacob, Kalob, and to those adopted into the tribe, Tamara, Coby, and photobomb guy, Dylan. My prayer is that each of them would be inspired to seek and to know truth and to know the God and author of it. To the reader, may the reading of these pages inspire, challenge, and bless you. Special thank you to my wife, Cassie, Pastor Tony Sanchez, Daniel Rubio, Ed Cardenas (my friend and author of *Lovito*, wonderful children's books), Daniel Tafoya (my atheist "test market" and new friend), and my kids for listening and giving feedback to the initial manuscript. May God bless our current families as He would bless our family from our former marriages. May He bless you, your kids, and your loved ones as you seek Him.

This work is published in a form that is a little rough to give the reader a sense of the authors passion for the message—as you read it, imagine the pages written in cursive or longhand, as a letter you have received from your Dad, your Grandfather, or that caring Uncle.

This is written on behalf of those I care for. If you are reading this and a worldwide event has just occurred, where hundreds of millions of people have disappeared and I am one of them, I can only imagine how crazy things are for you and for the world. First, let me say in simple language. What has occurred is the event declared in the Bible called by many the rapture of the church. It is vitally important that you understand the truth of this. Jesus Christ is the One prophesied about, and those taken were Christians—believers. We are the ones who, throughout all of history, put their faith and trust in Him. We are the ones who believed in our hearts and confessed with our mouths that Jesus died for our sins. We are those who had submitted ourselves to God's will, the ones who—through Christ with the help of the Holy Spirit—were made new creations.

It is vitally important you understand and listen to what I am saying. We are with Him now, awaiting the time we will return with Him. All people of all ethnicities from all nations heard a shout in the sky, the voice of an archangel, and all the world heard the last trumpet sound. Then the believers, those dead, raised from their graves first and then those who were living together were taken up, snatched up from all around the world in a moment to meet Him in the air. We will return with Him; we are His.

After a period, when He returns, people—great and small, those dead and those living who are not believers—will bend their knees to Him to face judgement. He will return with power and glory. He is returning to claim what is His.

Those around you are in great confusion. There is mayhem and anarchy taking hold all over. Panic and fear, like wildfire, again pours out over the earth. The authorities have declared a worldwide emergency. You have been conditioned to follow the narrative, to believe their experts and their sources without question. Those in control blame what has just happened on the extraterrestrials. There are aliens, just not the ones you think. The real aliens are not the ones the media has depicted. The real aliens are from interdimensional spiritual realms, not outer space. There are many groups of people all over the earth, including people from within governments who have been receiving ideas, guidance, and direction in concepts of new spirituality and new technology for many years.

In the United States, they inspired the development of many new scientific breakthroughs leading to the creation of a new race of beings. These are not new ideas; they have been here before; and they are a resurrected spawn. Their DNA is the result of the mingling of fallen angels with human DNA. They are entities created and enhanced by ancient demonic technology. These beings, these demigods are further improved by the combining of robotics and artificial intelligence. The idea of combining robotics, artificial intelligence with modified genetics is known as transhumanism. This concept started innocently enough. Each new advancement held the potential of curing disease, improving lifespans, or supplying new and improved limbs and other body parts to the crippled, the elderly, and the sick. The outcomes are anything but virtuous. These beings are the intended result. They are in the same way as those which existed prior to and just after the flood of Noah. They have been cloned, built, and resurrected. They are "the giants, men of old, the mighty men of renown" (Matthew 24:37). They are a tainted artificially created bloodline (Genesis 6:4). The Bible called them the Nephilim. They are the "hordes of hell," the titans. They are creatures, living on the earth, governed by Satan. As foretold, the earth once again knows transhuman organisms. Humans and angels mingled a race no longer merely human. These advancements give a sense of hope and promise. And like the echoes of events past, bloodlines become created. The result lead to wayward sexual behavior (Genesis 24).

Also prophesied, the earth has been experiencing episodes of extreme weather, diseases, famines, wars, ethnic conflicts and natural disasters, events increasing and pulsating, stronger and stronger in unison globally like the changes stirring in a woman's body prior to giving birth. One interconnected phenomenon converging toward the end known as globalization.

It is easy to see how early civilizations regarded these beasts as gods—gods who encouraged myths and ancient religions. It will be just as easy for those in control in your world now to convince countless peoples of their superiority and their divinity. This would seem like fantasy if it were not happening. You have been conditioned through myths, stories, media messages (in all forms). Years of ideas planted into your subconscious, ideas designed to confuse and distort your sense of good and evil. Programming used to deceive and convince there is no God, no heaven, no hell, no devil. Messages designed to harm you. Images and confusions of every sort flooded every sense, enticing the base impulses, saying over and over, "Live as you will. Do whatever you want. As long as you're not hurting anyone, nothing matters." You have also been trained, even taught, to not trust in God but to trust in yourself, your knowledge, your money, your job, your education, in the government, in evolution, in the media, in the occult, in the heroes of fantasy, in magic, in the freedom of the high, in nothing, or to trust in the aliens to come.

In the end, it did not matter which ideology you chose as "your own." They were all designed to mislead, to keep your focus off what really matters. It is vitally important you understand and listen to what I am saying. Mankind had been prepared for years for that day, conditioned, experimented on, hypnotized, lied to, entertained, and led down so many dead-end rabbit holes. We had all at times become confused and out of balance. We all lost our way and forgot our Creator. We were persuaded to hope in literally anything except Jesus and the God of the Bible. It is vitally important you understand and listen to what I am saying.

Air, water, and the food supply have been modified, manipulated, and polluted for many years. Many of the diseases and calamities perpetrated on the earth were crafted by artificial means. All these things were done to weaken our minds and bodies, decrease the population, disrupt the original design, and to prepare the masses to be dependent, manipulated, and controlled. Our population has been impacted by these things for so long that mankind has become frail and spiritually depraved. Men and women have been reduced to a shadow of who they were intended to be. Imagine how feeble we all look as we run from one selfish feel-good experience to the next. Then when real troubles come, because we lack strength and real depth of character, we only know to run to anyone, any experience, or any substance to hide or avoid facing any real challenge. We forgot our Creator wants us to cast our cares and burdens on Him.

Jesus (Matthew 24) himself said that when we see signs happening worldwide at the same time, the time of Him returning for His church is near. Jesus used the example of looking at the branches of a fig tree. To the ancient Jewish mind, the fig tree is where one went to find revelation from God. He basically said, "You hypocrites." Imagine calling the pope a hypocrite to his face. This is essentially what Jesus was doing as He spoke the religious leaders of his day, "You can tell by looking at the leaves of the fig tree when spring is coming, but you did not know the signs given to you [in Torah] to know of my coming." In other words, He was saying, "If you were aware and truly seeking God by talking to Him and taking time to read and understand the signs given to you in the ancient writings, you would know who I am." Jesus said that nations and people groups would rise in conflict against one another, and pestilence, famines, earthquakes, and great seismic events would happen in various places. When you see these things, he said, "You know that the time of my return is near." In other words, like the tree, with all the various branches getting ready to bloom at the same time, then the signs of what will happen next is clear. Like those religious leaders of Jesus day, anyone today, who took the time to examine the data would have known, these events had been happening simultaneously and worldwide with a measurable increase in severity and frequency since at least 1948.

The year 1948 is the date marking the rebirth of the state of Israel, a nation dead for two thousand years, a nation brought back to life in one day as predicted in the scriptures. It is also the date which started the time clock for the "first day of spring or the days of sorrows," the clock now ticking toward the end of days. Jesus said these events happening simultaneously would mark the time of His return for the Church. It would be like a woman in labor, awaiting the arrival of a child. The signs and pains would increase until His return like a child being born. The same events marking different and unique outcomes, one meant for good and the other for evil, one storm leading to destruction and the other to hope.

Maybe the combination of propaganda and our reactive nature, which pulls us toward fear, continually narrowed our focus and confused us a bit more each time after each new-world crisis. Perhaps this kept most blinded and tricked. The media has been successful in making people believe the severe weather and increases in earthquakes were solely the result of global warming, changing weather patterns, or just part of our evolving world, a living sphere where Mother Nature was upset with man's disregard of the earth. With each new pestilence or disaster, people held even tighter to this world. People in mass become more and more dependent, frightened, helpless, and reliant. Molded and misinformed for so long, even those who are the brightest or the most educated among you will find their hearts failing them in anguish as they come to realize the truth of the things coming and manifesting upon the earth. Every form evil can take; it has. It is vitally important you understand and listen to what I am saying.

Think about a dam holding back a great lake. This dam holds back and helps manage those things evil, harmful and destructive. It helps control and direct their movement. The dam, in this example, are those of us who have been taken. The church has been called salt and light. We were called this because we were changed inside as we trusted God and sought-after God's plans for us. We understood right and wrong, and we stood up for it. The simplest way to explain it is we were infused spiritually by Him, and we had a daily relationship with him. We were made righteous by his strength and power. By God's grace, we received the gift of salvation through faith in Him, the gift given to mankind by God. God the father poured Himself out into the form of a man, Jesus-Yeshua, and His life was given as the perfect sacrifice in substitution for man's sins. We were not perfect but were being perfected by the Holy Spirit. We loved God in spirit and in truth. We realized this world and our time in it was only temporary. We were infilled with the Holy Spirit. This allowed us to break free from the trappings of sin. We learned to submit to God's will, purposes, and direction for our lives. We learned our free will was totally free only as we communed with Him each day. We learned to genuinely love others without condition. This allowed us to be one, the body of Christ, as one throughout the world. Young and old, Jew and Gentile, former sinners of every sort, made white as snow by the blood shed on the cross. In other words, those taken were God's righteousness here on earth. In other words, our sin was forgiven. We were cleansed because we believed and accepted that Jesus had been the sacrifice for our sins, for the sins of the world. Now while we are gone, the dam has been broken. The flood coming is greater than the earth has ever seen or will ever see again.

Chances are you have heard some these tales before. The difference now is your living during the unfolding of events which are hard to grasp. Your survival forward depends on knowing and understanding the truth. I know it's confusing. You may be asking, "Who do I believe? Who do I listen to? What do I do?" It is vitally important you understand and listen to what I am saying.

Think about or reread the above statements. They are true.

The information and guidance coming to you next includes the world leader who seemingly can do miracles, bring world peace, the one who seems to have all the solutions. He is a false Christ. He is deception incarnate. He is the one led and empowered by the fallen one himself.

The world will quickly come under a one-world governmental system. The advances in medicine, the military, artificial intelligence, robotics, genetics, the digital monetary system, and the wealth of the world's economy are in his control and are at his disposal. He will bring solutions; they will lead to a false peace and a false hope. They seem right, don't they? He is a strong leader; he gives you a sense of hope, especially given the craziness of the event which recently took place. To get to where you at today, it took incredible survival skills. You may have had to do things. You never imagined you'd do to just to survive.

The temple in Jerusalem, if not already rebuilt as you read this, will soon be rebuilt. This world leader is a shadow of the true savior. He will claim to be the awaited messiah of every major world religion. In other words, he will convince all religions he is the awaited savior of the world. He is a liar, and there is no truth in him. He is accepted by most and declared the Savior of this world. In fact, he will soon sit in the temple and declare himself god. He is not. As in one collaborative effort, local municipalities will work with world leaders to "pull together as one humanity." Citizens, the world over will be compelled to "come together as one people, to be tolerant and accepting during these trying times." The world has a universal religion accepted by many. Nearly all in the world will be so desperate for answers. They will easily bow and submit to the new requirements for worship and to the demands of their new savior. It is vitally important you understand and listen to what I am saying. Your life, your true life, depends on it.

If you are still reading this, you are the remnant, the true resistance. You are those who know in your inner self, God and His Son. Jesus is your savior. You can sense Him. He is the Lord of all creation, the Lord of lords, and the King of kings. He became flesh. All things made were made through Him and by Him. He is the beginning and the end. You may not fully understand this, but somehow you know that He is calling you. Somehow you know it is true.

Take this letter and print it. Keep it safely hidden in order to share it and reference it. If you can find a Bible and you need more evidence, I've included references and online resources for you to look up and research what I am telling you.

Other events which will take place. There will be two witnesses sent by God in bodily physical form to proclaim that God is God, He alone is salvation, and He alone is peace. The world will see and hear their message. They will be killed, and their bodies will be left on display as an example of what happens to those who challenge the global system of the supreme leader. People throughout the earth will be so fooled; they will celebrate their deaths and trade gifts. They will be resurrected in three days. There will even be angels preaching about Jesus's return in the skies at this point in history. Many from the remnant of all cultures will come to believe in Jesus as their Savior, the Christ. There will be a remnant from the tribes of Israel, 144,000 strong. They will have God's mark on their foreheads. They will proclaim the Messiah boldly without seeing death.

Please understand. Accepting God as your salvation at this point and acknowledging Jesus at this time will bring you physical death. You will be hunted and killed "for pronouncing such lies." Those around you will accept a mark on their right hands and/or on their foreheads. Many will be dumbfounded and will receive the mark willingly. A chip perhaps. It is a way, the only way, to buy and sell any goods for anyone anywhere in the world. This is a ploy; it is a way for the power construct for the elite to track and control everyone. Accepting Christ as Savior at this point will earn you endless life with Him. As you do this, you will be filled with the Holy Spirit, the same power which raised Jesus from the dead. It will be like blinders or scales falling off your eyes. Fear and worry will be replaced with love. Seek God's direction, and He himself will give you your marching orders. You will win many for Him. For there are many like you, many who are a remnant, many who resist. It is vitally important you understand and listen to what I am saying.

Do not take the mark on your body. It is more than a mark of allegiance, more than just the newest technology. It is total submission, a giving of yourself over, to this false savior and his counterfeit system. Don't be fooled. The peace the world now has is false and will not stand or last. Those who take the mark have lost their souls already, and there is not hope for them. Their souls are lost to eternity with the devil and his fallen ones in the lake of fire in hell. Hell is a real place. It was not prepared for or designed for man or mankind. The mark somehow fundamentally changes you, and you completely lose your free will. More importantly, you lose your soul. Many have already chosen their fate by not making an informed choice for Christ. Many of these will confirm this by taking the mark. They will spend eternity in the lake of fire, eternally separated from the God who created them.

Recognize! God alone is salvation. Christ alone is the door or the way to salvation. The Holy Spirit alone will sustain and guide you. The Bible only is the celestial message to man, the only holy book to predict the future with 100 percent accuracy. If you've accepted Christ at this point as your Lord, He has sealed you with His holy spirit. At present, you are having eternal life with Him in His coming kingdom. Salvation means you live, you truly live. Death has no hold on you. Choosing Christ ensures your life on this earth will be lived out as a sacrifice. Your sacrifice will have its great rewards like the death of any soldier who has fallen for his or her friends or for the greater good. As a believer in Christ the Messiah, the King of kings, you will be killed. You will be like the ancient saints. You will be martyred for your faith and your beliefs. Don't be troubled in your hearts. You will be with Him and be renewed in your new body, and you will return with Him. When this happens, the second resurrection of the dead will happen. All will come before the judgment of God. All will bow before their maker. All words, intentions, and works will be judged. Those covered by the blood will receive "crowns of righteousness." All works will be tested and tried. All evil not covered by Christ's work on the cross will be burned up. Those not His have chosen their lot in the lake of fire with the devil and the angels that fell with him. Jesus will return with all of those who have understood who He is. The world, the earth, is expecting her true King. When He returns, He will rule this earth from the new Jerusalem, the new city which will descend from the heavens, and He will rule and reign on this earth with His saints for a thousand years. He will establish a perfect world government.

When you see the false one—a man who leads the world out of the sorrows and chaos, a man who will be mortally injured, a man who will simulate a resurrection, one who will create an entity, a modern-day prophet, a living being with solutions, who possess all knowledge and has no soul—he (they) will seem like the savior. Many will worship them as their awaited Krishna, enlightened one, Messiah, Jesus (PBUH), and the Imam Al-Mahdi. The religious will each individually and collectively believe he is the embodiment of their unique and individual awaited savior, their god, their messiah. The man was born in the area of the Golan Heights, north of Jerusalem, and he will claim to be a descendant of the Jews. He will declare to love the land of Israel above all else. He is a liar and incapable of truth; there is no truth in him. The third temple will be rebuilt in Jerusalem. Then when this happens, when this world leader sits in the third temple in Jerusalem, and when he appeals to the people of the world for worldwide worship of himself, when he declares himself god, when this happens, when he defiles the temple, when he sits in the temple in Jerusalem, the world will have had exactly three and a half years of unprecedented world peace, a worldwide calm, a new earth, fresh beginnings of a newfound promise.

Count forward from the time he declares himself god and sits it the temple. If you break the years into days at this point, you can calculate the following events to the day. In the last three and a half years, there will be a great hardship on the world, tribulation, the likes which have never been nor will ever be again. The events you have experienced up to this point, all you have witnessed and lived through, all the craziness is but a foreshadow, the tip of a wicked iceberg of troubles to come.

Hundreds of millions of people from every race and every nation have vanished. It was not the aliens. This will create a worldwide turmoil. It will impact everything. The whole world will be primed and ready to accept their new savior. First three and a half years of his worldwide reign brings peace and immense hopefulness. The rest of the iceberg, the last three and a half years, ushers in great turmoil and distress on the earth. It will be like an Avenger's movie meets the night of living dead. A time of confusion and fear, a time where it will be hard to determine if the good guys are good or if the seemingly evil villain is really the good guy. "He's the good guy, right?" It is a deception, a lie.

The problems of the earth have been mostly solved up to this point, including reaching peace in the Middle East. He has given the world new ways and wonderful solutions, including salvaging and resurrecting the world's economy. He is awe-inspiring, he is a great orator, he is pleasing to look at but does not honor the loving touch of a woman, and he is powerful, magical, and motivational. He utilizes technology like no one before him. The artificial intelligence he has created is alive, and it has solutions too. His creation is like a god. Together, they control AI soldiers and other beings who have been formed, many who are like the superheroes, except these guys are real; they are the titans and gods of old.

Answers that work. All is good, all is getting stabilized, and all are received and recognized and marked. There is great hope for extending life, the superrich have already achieved transhuman advancements and seem to have reached immortality. "There is not good or right. Accept what we believe, right?" All are known. "Love is love, and family is family. Decide who and what you are. Do what's right for you. This is good, right?" Take the chip or mark on your hand or forehead so that you can buy and sell and be part of the new future. Truly be "all that you were created to be." "Be a team player." "We are in this together. Our savior has solved the problems of the world." "Right?" "He's the good guy?" "Right?" It is vitally important you understand and listen to what I am saying.

Take a moment to breathe right now and think about how fleeting this moment is.

Understand you and I are nothing more than a creation. Dust formed into life by the Creator of the universe. Even those who seek after alternative routes to prolonging life, those who seek to prolong life by synthetically infusing strange flesh with computer and machine have an end. None of us is God. We do not have the right to play God or to define what is right or what is good. God alone is good. His ways are not our ways, and His thoughts are above our thoughts. God loves you. God, Creator Spirit, humbled Himself to become like His creation to provide a way to pay for the sin of mankind. Jesus is the embodiment of life and truth. He is the model for us. Our healing, our salvation, and our blessings come through a humbling of ourselves. Stop for a moment because I know that most of you have heard some or all of this before. Understand and listen.

There is a God, the Father, who is Spirit. He and He alone is Holy. He is three in one. Like light when it passes through a prism is divided into different colors, one God, three expressions, one light, one God. He is your salvation. Don't take my word for it. Talk to Him. Take any question to Him. Take any doubt to Him. As you do this, He will make Himself known to you, known in ways which will satisfy all questions or uncertainty you may have. He is living, He is truth, and He is life. His plans for you are good. He created you for a purpose. He desires a relationship with you. "The God who created the universe desires a relationship with me?" Yes, the one who hung the stars knows you. He knows every tear you have ever cried. He understands sorrow, grief, rejection, and pain. He is acquainted with your struggles. He knows these things because He experienced them as Christ. God is the essence of living. He cannot be ended. Jesus said he was life. He is the beginning, and before Him was nothing. He is the author of this end. Life with God does not end. Death is the result of sin, the fall in this life. Jesus conquered death; His shed blood blots out and covers sin, and through him, you can have living, real life.

We all die. Don't fear death. Fear only the One who has the power over your soul. We all have an eternal existence. Fear living eternally away from the One who loves you. The world's system is demonic. The evil one does not care about you in this life, and he does not care if you spend eternity in hell. Jesus told us of the things coming. He told us who He was. The ancient writings foretold of who He was. His life and death changed the known world. His words remain true, even those inspired and written 750 years before his birth like those found of Him in Isaiah 53. He is and was. Spirit became flesh and dwelt among us so that we could be redeemed. The beginning of wisdom is a healthy fear or regard, for He who is all knowing, all creative, all loving, and all powerful (Proverbs 9). Like my wife used to say, "I get it. He turned some chick into salt. That's enough for me to understand the power of God."

Messiah is calling you, "Come to me, all you who are weary and burdened, and I will give you rest. Take my yoke upon you and learn from me, for I am gentle and humble in heart, and you will find rest for your souls. For my yoke is easy and my burden is light" (Matthew 11:28–30 NIV).

I always wondered what that verse meant. Have you ever seen a group of horses tied together, pulling an old wagon train or stagecoach? The yoke is the piece of wood allowing the horses to pull together as one. When I surrendered my life and every area of it to

God, when I yoked with him. Even the troubles or hardship I went through when I cried out to Him and put my trust in Him always worked out for my good. As I learned to trust this more, it was easy. Exciting even. I did not always know where I was being led. As I learned to trust Him each step of the way, I learned He was my shelter and ever-present help in times of trouble. I learned that when I found balance with Him, my will was in order. I learned purposes and abilities I did not know I had. This letter to you today is an example of that. When I was a young man, attending University, I had an English professor once tell me, "Your writing isn't just bad. It's so bad that I don't see you finishing college or ever completing an advanced degree." I was stubborn enough to work through each piece of writing necessary to complete several degrees, but I never thought I would be used in a way to reach others. I never thought I would have inspiration to even write such a letter as I write to you now.

Are you still resisting? Do you feel his tug? He knocks on the door of our hearts. He talks to us in the still small voice. He was there for you and has been there for you so many times before. He heard your prayers. Once you got a no or wait for an answer, you became angry with Him. When He answered your prayer and things just worked out once again, you ignored Him. If you take a moment to be reflective, contemplative, and honest, look back, and you will see the times He was there. Surrendering to Him feels scary, I know. Do not worry about what you have done. None of us alone is good enough, so stop trying to be. His love will complete the emptiness you feel inside of you, the space you have tried to fill up on your own with all sorts of things. Ask, seek, find, and believe.

Am I asking you to trust and give yourself over to someone and something you cannot even see? Facts can change. Truth remains. Seek it out. If it is true, it can be found. We did not have a blind faith. We had a faith based on the substance of the life and future we hoped for. We had a faith based on the evidences of the things we cannot see (Hebrews 11:1). Did you catch that? Even the scriptures tell us to seek the evidences of those things you cannot see. Can you imagine the early disciples running around telling people about their teacher, "This guy, Jesus, yeah, he healed and did this amazing stuff.

He is the awaited Christ. Yeah, the Messiah, the one foretold. Yeah, they killed him and hung him on a tree, and He rose from the dead?"

Would anyone believe any of this without evidences? Did they make this up to make their guy fit the expectations? Would His followers even have followed Him if He did not fit what was foretold of who the Christ would be? Would later followers be willing to be dipped into oil or wax to be set on fire or fed to lions, ripped apart in coliseums, stabbed, stoned, and beheaded, etc. for a fabrication? Yes, there are groups who have been willing to die for a lie in the past (The Kamikaze's), and like all groups willing to die for their cause, they believed their cause to be true. Look around you now. What is happening? Does it fit Jesus's words? Is it measurable?

In His time, the proof was captured by firsthand accounts of healings and miracles of all sort, facts eyewitnesses saw with their own eyes, testimonials of those times of the coming Christ, and words ringing true of these times, words written hundreds, thousands of years before which manifested and are coming into existence in precise detail in this time. As I write this, my wife and I discuss current events. We just received a letter from her brother. The letter is packed with information correlating pandemics and pestilences on the earth since the turn of the century. I share her words with you for thought and to make you smile. "I don't, don't gotta read nothin', just watch the news and look around. There's proof all around you. Open your eyes." (Now read her words again, hearing her West Texan drawl combined with some Oklahoma heritage, raised on a ranch in Southern New Mexico, in the country mixed with a bit of hard living as a youth.) I love how she says much with few words.

Other proofs include everyone throughout all of time who has believed on His name and has experienced deep personal change, the drug addict to a person of sobriety and the hater to a person of humility and love. Jesus brought change to me and to my life in ways I hardly believe at times. Anyway, that was then; now the evidence is in front of us.

Take a moment to breathe right now and think about how fleeting this moment is.

Understand you and I are nothing more than a creation. Dust formed into life by the Creator of the universe. Even those who seek after alternative routes to prolonging life, those who seek to extend life by artificially infusing strange flesh with computers and machines have an end. None of us is God. We do not have the right to play God or to define what is right or what is good. God alone is good. His ways are not our ways, and His thoughts are above our thoughts. God loves you. He (God) humbled Himself to become like His creation to provide a way to pay for the sin of mankind; to pay for your sins. Jesus is the embodiment of life and truth. He is the model for us. Our healing, our salvation, and our blessings come through a humbling of ourselves. Stop for a moment because I know that most of you have heard some of or all of this before. Understand and listen.

There is a God in heaven. He is in control. He is your salvation. Talk to Him. As you do this, He will make Himself significant and known to you. He will answer your questions in ways satisfying any question or doubt you may have.

We all die. Do not fear death. Fear only the One who has the power over your soul. Fear living eternally away from the One who loves you. The world's system is demonic. The evil one does not care about you as you live this life, and he does not care if you spend eternity in hell.

As in the days of Noah, these are the days of echoes past, a time of turmoil and unrest. The first destruction was by water, then the times since Christ, our taking away, His second return and the judgement, establishing a reign on this earth for one thousand years, then the final destruction will be by fire, then a new heaven and a new earth. The Arc and means of escape for you is Christ. I pray you find life in the middle of the storm and hope through every sort of sorrow.

Do not take my word for any of this since my words alone do not have any power. If you have heard His call and answered it, seek to learn more and to be closer to Him. If you sense Him calling you and you are fearful and hesitant to act, your eyes still focused on the troubles raging around you, know His perfect love cast out all fear. Seek truth; it exists to be found.

If you still can find a Bible, research what I am telling you. Ask yourself, "Can hope really be found in the middle of a storm? Does evidence exist to show me what is true? What did the ancient church fathers really teach? What does the Bible really teach? Are modern-day events, the exact fulfillment of what the prophets, and what Yeshua taught thousands of years ago? Does the old testament really testify of Him? What is truth? If I objectively looked just at the data generated from modern-day events, what questions would I be left with?"

I have included Bible references and other resources for you to check out for yourself. Finally ask, "What does this all mean for me?"

It is vitally important you understand and listen to what I am saying. Your life in eternity depends on it.

I love you, guys.

R Joseph Romero,
03/16/2020

As I write this, the coronavirus is spreading quickly throughout the world and the United States. Here in Albuquerque, New Mexico—my city and state, like most other cities and states—the people and the state of New Mexico are under a government stay home order. Travel is restricted, and the way we shop has been impacted. Some of the most populated cities and states throughout the US are being hit the hardest. Churches and nonessential business are closed. People are hooding food, toilet paper, and other supplies. There is fear and panic in the air as the US government just approved the largest stimulus package in US history to an attempt to minimize the coming economic fallout on the United States. The world is at a standstill. The number of people infected is growing exponentially. The worldwide death toll is also on the rise. Local governments are more and more looking to national and world leaders for assistance, help, and direction. World leaders like the UN are in the process of developing plans and suggestions to help stabilize the world economy. Our systems of medicine and economics have been negatively impacted. I hear people talking about a return to normal. I do not believe there will be a return to what was prior to COVID-19. Like the outcomes of the events of 9/11, which ushered in a new normal, the results of COVID-19 will bring new changes worldwide. The US economy and the economy of the world may never be the same. This season may pass, but the times to come have been forever impacted by COVID-19.

Bible References/Other Resources to Check Out

Did you know approximately one-third of the Bible speaks of rapture and the end times?

Some of the Bible references: Daniel 12:1–2, 1 Thessalonians 4:16–18, 1 Thessalonians 5:1–8, Luke 17:34–37, Revelations 3:10, Mark 13:5–8, Mark 24:32, Matthew 24:31, Luke 10:20, Luke 12:40, Matthew 24:37, Luke 13:6–9, Luke17:34, Philippians 3:20–21, Romans 8:18–19, Acts 1:7–8, 1 Corinthians 15:51–53, 2 Corinthians 5:10, John 14:3, Revelations 20:2–5, Revelations 3:10, Revelations 11:15–19, Isaiah 53.

Extra Bible Sources

The End Times by Ancient Church Fathers by Dr. Ken Johnson on YouTube. (These are lectures summarizing the writings from the disciples of the disciples, "the ancient church fathers.") According to Dr. Johnson, "The early church fathers' teaching on the end times were all consistent" and changes in doctrinal interpretation did not drastically change until the third and fourth centuries. Many of these later writings influenced modern church doctrine. I found Dr. Johnson's resources professionally researched and presented. Dr. Johnson has many resources and books available; I highly recommend any serious searcher investigates his books and presentations.

Koinonia House. Lectures and studies presented by Chuck Missler on YouTube. (Koinonia House has many resources on many subjects, including end times, and others based on more modern developments of physics, math, genetics, artificial intelligence, UFOs, etc.

Now the End Begins on YouTube, an ongoing list of world headlines as they align to Bible prophesy as done since 2009.

The Chosen, the first original TV series about Jesus Christ, VidAngle studios.

Convergence of the End Times Signs (movie) on YouTube, 2015. (Signs of the last days happening worldwide at the same time: economic, scientific, technologic, cultural, geopolitical, and moral. This film is well done. It is the first I had ever seen that allows the viewer to see the evidence and its comparison to scripture from the Bible for themselves without forcing the religious part. It challenges the viewer to see and think about the data.)

Earthquakes.com. (Tracs worldwide, earthquake activity from a 1.5 magnitude and greater from "today" back.) Research for yourself. Are these happening more often and with greater frequency as the Bible predicts? For example, today, April 1, 2020, there have been 174 earthquakes in the last twenty-four hours, 1,024 in the past seven days, 4,719 in the past thirty days, and 63,330 in the last 356 days. I'd be curios as how to these numbers compare to when you may be checking these stats.

Earthquakes.usgs.gov. (Daily information on earthquakes, magnitude, and location.)

Https://ourworldindata.org/famines (Data tracked of worldwide famines since 1860).

East Africa's plagues and the bizarre climate. www.nationalgeographic.com.

After coronavirus, locus could be the next plagues to hit China. http//www.the dailybeast.com

Plague of locusts threatens East African economies as UN sounds alarm. http//www.cnbc.com/2020

"A Plague of Locusts, Earthquakes in Diverse Places, and Weather That Has Gone Completely Nuts." http//wwwthedailycoin.org

Live free online volcanic eruption Map-Radar Tracker Radartracker.com/volcano_eruptions

"God loves you. It does not matter what you have done. He sent His son. He died for you. Ask Him to be the lord of your life. There is no right prayer. Simply cry out to God. Talk to Him. Say something like, 'God, forgive me for my sins against You. I believe and accept Jesus died on the cross for me and for the forgiveness of my sins. Fill me with Your Holy Spirit and with Your love. Help me to find Your will for my life.'"

"If you declare with your mouth, 'Jesus is Lord,' and believe in your heart that God raised him from the dead, you will be saved" (Romans 10:9 NIV).

If you have prayed this prayer, find a Bible-believing congregation of believers and a Bible as you still can.

May God bless you.

About the Author

R. Joseph Romero devoted his twenty-eight-year career in Education to helping others develop skills necessary to enrich their lives. In his words, "I became hooked to helping others, back as a substitute teacher. There is nothing like seeing the light bulb go on for someone when they've learned something new." After obtaining an advanced degree, R. Joseph worked as a special education teacher, school administrator, and district level administrator. R. Joseph has bachelor's degrees in psychology and sociology and has a master's degree is in special education. R. Joseph also trained staff within Native American (BIA) contract and reservation schools in New Mexico and Eastern Arizona.

Writing *The Days of Echoes Past: Hope through the Storm* came about after examining the written accounts of the ancient church fathers as summarized through lectures given by historian, Dr. Ken Johnson, studying scripture, binge-watching *The Chosen* by Dallas Jenkins, rediscovering lectures by Chuck Missler (Koinonia House), prayer, reading *The Book of Mysteries* by Jonathan Cahn, and by seeking God's direction daily.

Like all gifted teachers, R. Joseph believes a teacher's primary role is to create a (safe) space to allow the learner to experience the tension between the known and unknown, concepts necessary for a reader (or student) to be challenged enough to want to delve into and discover the truth of a subject. The most sacred teaching position he has continues to be found within his role as a parent.

CPSIA information can be obtained
at www.ICGtesting.com
Printed in the USA
LVHW110427030221
678219LV00007B/701